47 Amazing Things to See and Do in Colombia

Neil Bennion

47 AMAZING THINGS TO SEE AND DO IN
COLOMBIA

Contents

About This Book

A few years ago I went to Colombia to learn how to dance. During that time I travelled extensively, spending over half a year there and exploring much of what the country had to offer. I wrote a book about the dance journey – Dancing Feat: One Man's Mission to Dance Like a Colombian – but I felt like I still had a lot left to share about this amazing land, so I decided to write another book. And this is it.

Colombia is a hugely diverse country in terms of people, culture and landscape. It has so much just waiting to be discovered by those who take the chance to go and visit. And I'm going to share some of the highlights with you here.

This book is at its heart a list of things to see and do. If you want to get a more in-depth feel for Colombia and its people — and have a laugh at my expense while you're doing so — then consider checking out my other book, Dancing Feat (http://amzn.to/1odeSVE).

Anyway, that's quite enough chatter — let's get on with it.

A Quick History Lesson

The history of any country is a complex thing that cannot simply be reduced to a few paragraphs. But what the heck, let's have a go anyway.

Back in the day, the area of land we now call Colombia was populated by lots of different tribes who were just kind of chilling out and making cool-looking stuff out of gold. These were the indigenous people of the Americas, or Amerindians as they're sometimes known. They probably came down from the Caribbean and more northerly parts of the Americas a long time earlier.

Around the year 1498, the Spanish arrived on boats from Europe and proceeded to gallivant through the land, bringing peace and harmony wherever they went (sarcasm alert), and leaving a flower-like scent trail behind them. Assuming that the rotting cadavers of fallen indigenous people smell like flowers, that is.

The Spanish brought with them Catholicism, slaves from Africa and precious foreign diseases, and took away large quantities of gold. As their population increased, racial mixing occurred — after all, it must get kind of lonely if you're a member of a European colonising force that has neglected to include many women. With multiple races now occupying the same lands, the Spanish enforced a kind of racial caste system, generously placing themselves at the top. But as the *criollo* population (those of Spanish ancestry, but born locally) began to increase, so did resentment at the privileges of those born in mainland Spain, as well as the control and influence of Spain in general.

Eventually, people took up arms over this, with the result that Colombia became independent in 1810. And then again in 1819. It was kind of messy like that. Indeed, things weren't truly concluded until about 1823.

Monument to Símon Bolívar, 'The Liberator', at Puente de Boyacá

Independence might have been won, but political stability would remain more elusive, with the two main sides — Liberal and Conservative — bickering constantly, and even engaging in armed conflict. Things never fully calmed down, and, in 1949, furore over the murder of a Liberal Party presidential candidate quickly escalated into long-term countrywide violence and retribution — a truly appalling period of time known as La Violencia (The Violence).

In the era following this, social inequality spurred the

formation of left-wing guerrilla groups like the FARC (Revolutionary Armed Forces of Colombia). These were followed into existence by right-wing paramilitary groups, which emerged to protect the interests of landowners and others from said guerrillas. Then, just to really stir things up, the drugs trade rose to prominence.

In the 1990s, the main cartels were broken up, and, from a peak at the turn of the century, the country's rates of serious crime gradually started to come down. As a direct consequence, the country has now re-emerged as not only a safer place for most Colombians, but also a realistic (not to mention fantastic) destination for tourists, bringing us to where we are today.

An Even Quicker Geography Lesson

Colombia has everything. Not content with a coastline on both the Pacific and the Atlantic Oceans, it also has a slice of the Amazon (the world's largest rainforest), three cordilleras of the Andes mountains, two mighty valleys, hugely expansive plains and even a desert. And, with the altitude varying so much, it also has a wide range of eco-systems, with all the associated diversity in flora and fauna (that's plants and animals, for those not acquainted with guidebook parlance).

Please excuse me the vanity of quoting from my own book, Dancing Feat:

"It's the place where South America begins; where Central America's dwindling bough suddenly engorges into a full-on trunk; where the great mountainous spine of the Americas explodes into the swashbuckling horde of peaks, plateaus and volcanoes known as the Andes. It's also the place that took on the name of that great explorer Christopher Columbus, the man who would have discovered the Americas had some other people (the Vikings) not discovered them first, and had there not also been a whole bunch of people living there already."

Is Colombia Safe?

It's a common question, based on a widely-held perception of what Colombia is like.

So is it safe? Well the question most people really want answering is "Is it safe enough to travel around?" And the answer to that is — yes, absolutely.

However, that answer does come with a 'but', so let's go into the situation in more detail.

The headline problems, such as long-term kidnapping, are at levels a fraction of what they were at their peak in 2000. And the country's homicide rate in 2014 was the lowest in decades (although at 12,800 for the year, still not exactly insignificant).

Street crime, however, is an issue in many towns and cities. We're talking about everything from pickpocketing and bag snatching to knife-point muggings and the spiking of drinks, or even the *paseo millonario*, where a rogue taxi driver and accomplice take you on a forced ATM tour of the city. And despite the recent to-ing and fro-ing in peace negotiations, entire regions of the country are still no-go zones.

What does this mean to you?

It simply means to take care. Check out the current situation using up-to-date sources like the UK's foreign travel advice pages (http://bit.ly/1uzGY3s), or those provided by your own country's government. Travel in numbers. Don't leave your drink unattended, nor accept one from someone you don't know well enough. Seek local advice on where is safe and not safe to go — it can sometimes vary on a street-by-street basis. Call for taxis — or get your guest house or hotel to do it for you —

rather than hailing them on the street. Avoid running with scissors. Don't walk about at night unless you know for sure it's okay to do so.

I meant what I said about the scissors.

Remember that Colombia is not a good country for off-the-beaten-track adventure. I strongly suggest you read the article Some Travelers to Colombia are Plain Stupid by journalist and hostel-owner Richard McColl (http://bit.ly/1ErVLCg). And check out this map (http://bit.ly/1uzGY3s) of okay and not-so-okay places, issued by the UK FCO. Also keep an eye out for naturally-occurring issues like erupting volcanoes and the like. If you see people running away from one then try and keep up. Yes, I'm being flippant — you can't outrun pyroclastic flow any more than you can surf molten lava. So best just to steer clear.

Of course, I can't tell you about all the possible dangers you might encounter and, besides, things change quickly in the world. It's up to you to do your own research, and to always check with the relevant people, that what you're doing is okay. So if you stab yourself in the eye with a *chorizo* sausage because the coach hit a bump in the road, then don't come crying to me. Yes, that's a disclaimer.

The most important thing, though, is that you don't let any of this put you off visiting what is an amazing country inhabited by, for the most part, incredibly friendly and giving people.

And finally, just make sure you remember that it's Colombia, not Columbia*, or you'll completely deserve any ills that befall you.

*Just to complicate matters, 'pre-Columbian' is perfectly fine.

Maps

THE COASTAL REGIONS

Caribbean Sea

Punta Gallinas 14

Cabo de la Vela 14

Riohacha

La Guajira

Santa Marta   Taganga 13

Bocas De Ceniza 4

Tayrona National Park 11

Barranquilla 1

Ciudad Perdida 5

Volcan del Totumo 2

Minca 10

Nabusimake 17

Cartagena 9

Valledupar 6

Isla del Rosario 15

Islas de San Bernardo 15

Tolú 8

Mompós 7

PANAMA   Capurganá 12

El Banco 3

VENEZUELA

River Cauca

Cúcuta

Bucaramanga

Barrancabermeja 3

Medellín

Pacific Ocean   Bahia Solano 16

River Magdalena

1 — Go Carnival-crazy in Barranquilla

Let's get one thing clear: Carnival is a colossal pain in the backside in many ways. All the transport in and out of the city is fully booked, accommodation is three times the regular price — if you can find any — and entire streets are blocked off, making navigating some parts of the city pretty tricky. But let's get something else clear — it's absolutely worth it.

The carnival at Barranquilla is said to be the second biggest carnival in the world after the one in Rio de Janeiro, Brazil. The main focus is the planned parades, consisting of gigantic fantasy floats, extravagant costumes and a wall of noise. Dancers sashay their way down the street in displays of the many different musical genres that represent Colombia — everything from jazzy nightclub-esque salsa to folkloric styles such as the garabato, where death itself makes an appearance. Meanwhile, people in the crowd — wearing the *sombrero vueltiao* (the iconic hat of Colombia), comedy sunglasses and the like — attack each other with spray-foam and cornflour.

To experience Carnival, you can just show up at wherever that day's festivities are taking place and stand in the free viewing area by the side of the road. You'll definitely feel a part of what's going on that way. But it's worth noting that festivals tend to attract opportunistic pickpockets and other ne'er do wells. Indeed, a common ruse is for thieves to spray foam in your face and then go through your pockets while you're disorientated. A better option, especially if you plan to take a camera, is to book a place in a *palco* — one of the giant road-side stands.

And there are other threats – during my own time in Carnival, I got dragged up from my seat in the stand by a local who insisted I dance cumbia with her to the rhythms of the band (every *palco* has its own group). If this kind of thing happens to you, there's no getting out of it — just go with the flow and enjoy it, and they'll love you for it.

Cumbia dancers at Barranquilla's Carnival

2 — Slop around in mud at Volcan del Totumo

The mud volcano is a phenomenon present in various parts of the world, and one of those places is Colombia's Caribbean coast, where there are quite a few dotted about.

Experiencing one is something that truly has to be done to be appreciated. You can't feel the bottom, yet you aren't sinking. You're floating, although you have no sense of buoyancy. You're just there. You're not 'stuck' per se as you can move your limbs freely — it's just that any kind of lateral progress is slow to the point of hilarity.

Indeed, I was originally going to call this section 'swim in a mud volcano', but this would perhaps give the wrong impression, suggesting as it does a noticeable rate of bodily propulsion, when in fact you're mostly just flapping about gloopily on the spot.

The best-known mud volcano is Volcan del Totumo — you can arrange to go on a tour there through various hostels and agencies in Cartagena. It's not the only one, however: I visited one near the village of San Antero, joining those locals that also felt Sunday afternoons were best spent half-submerged in goo.

There's generally a fee for access to these places, and the washer women — who hose you down once you slither back out — also need paying.

3 — Follow the conquistadors upriver from El Banco

Whilst the mighty Amazon River does brush Colombia's outer fringes, the real general in river terms is the Magadalena, which plunders its way through the heart of the country before discharging, nearly a thousand miles from its source, at Bocas de Ceniza (see #4).

With the railways mostly gone, almost all intercity transport in Colombia nowadays is done via car, coach or plane. But if you fancy something a bit less ordinary, try taking the public boat service between the towns of El Banco and Barrancabermeja. It's far from comfortable — you're crammed in a confined space for hours on end, and it's not like you can get up and take a walk — but it's a great opportunity to see the country from a different perspective.

The Magdalena River at Barrancabermeja

There are historical elements to this journey, too. It's roughly the same route that the conquistador Gonzalo Jiménez de Quesada took in heading inland in 1536, and it was also a major trade route for many years. This, despite the fact that, prior to the arrival of steamboats, it took a bare minimum of 25 days to get between Honda (near Bogotá) and the coast.

Nowadays, this (admittedly shorter) journey takes roughly seven or eight hours upstream — or did on my visit — and downstream, in the opposite direction, is even quicker, for obvious reasons.

The Barrancabermeja end is well-connected by road — coaches run to Bucaramanga up in the Andes, for example, taking a couple of hours. At the El Banco end, however, the land is riddled with swamps and channels, meaning that transport is infrequent and getting around is a bit more of an adventure. People generally use Mompós as a stopover, which you would be well advised to do, as it's a great place to visit in its own right (see #7).

4 — Explore Bocas de Ceniza on a *trencito*

Bocas de Ceniza is the place at which the mighty Magdalena River finally makes it out to open sea at Barranquilla. It's also the name of the long breakwater which separates the river and the sea — something which was constructed in 1936 as part of works to make the final part of the river navigable, turning the city of Barranquilla into a sea port.

Along the breakwater run rickety little *trencitos* — open-frame railway vehicles — carrying visitors out onto the narrow limb between the two bodies of water. En route you pass little wooden buildings in faded pastel shades. Indeed, the whole place has that sense of abandoned seaside town about it, albeit a seaside town that is also a riverside town. As you get further out, you pass ramshackle fishermen's huts, the track ultimately breaking up into a trail of rocks festooned with abandoned flip-flops and other discarded bits and pieces.

Bocas de Ceniza presents a fascinating visual anomaly, with the grey of the silty river on one side and the blue of the open sea on the other. At the rocky end point, you may even be able to see the one blooming into the other.

It's also a good place to go for lunch, as there is a plethora of fish restaurants at the start of the breakwater. When I visited, there was even a little shack serving food way out on the breakwater itself. And you certainly know the fish is fresh since you can see the fishermen for yourself sitting out on rocks, the spray coating them in a patina of salt.

The easiest way to get to Bocas de Ceniza is by taxi from Barranquilla. You may have to wait for the *trencito* to be full of passengers before it will head out along the breakwater, though alternatively you may be able to take a *moto* (motorcycle taxi) out there. Although note that railway tracks were not designed to have motorbikes running down the middle of them, and your innards might not thank you for the choice. Mine have still to come to a rest.

5 — Hike to ancient ruins at Ciudad Perdida

La Ciudad Perdida (The Lost City) is one of the country's premier tourist attractions, with many seeing it as Colombia's answer to Machu Picchu.

It's a reasonable comparison. Both are the ancient ruins of settlements built by indigenous people in pre-colonial times. Both are in remote locations and were 'discovered' relatively recently (Machu Picchu in 1911, Ciudad Perdida in 1972). Both were apparently already known of by locals. And both offer paying visitors the chance to go charging on up to them in a flurry of goretex and ripping velcro.

Trekking through the jungle to Ciudad Perdida

One contrasting element, though, is visitor numbers — the figures for Ciudad Perdida are a tiny fraction of those for Machu Picchu. Whilst another is that, for Ciudad Perdida, you don't really have any option other than to go on a multi-day trek to reach the site (Machu Picchu can be done as a day trip).

It's not an easy hike up to the ruins at Ciudad Perdida, but it's very worthwhile, not just for the vista that greets you at the climax, but for the whole experience — you spend several days heading through jungle-clad mountains, passing tribes of indigenous people on reservations, wading through streams and playing sweary card games with your fellow hikers.

The trek can only be done via organised tour, which at the time of writing cost 600,000 COP (about 310 US dollars). Tours are generally four or five days long, with accommodation in hammocks and mattresses en route. Choose what equipment you take carefully, as it involves a mixture of jungle trekking and splashing through streams, and the humidity means things take forever to dry.

6 — Learn to love the accordion in Valledupar

Not many people who visit Colombia ever go to Valledupar, but pretty much everyone will get to hear the music most strongly associated with the city — *vallenato*. It's played in most parts of the country, and on the Caribbean coast it's ubiquitous. You hear it in every cafe, taxi and nightclub. It's completely inescapable.

Shame, then, that many visitors are either ambivalent about it or even dislike it. I was certainly no fan myself, but then I went to Valledupar's Festival de la Leyenda Vallenata (Vallenato Legend Festival), and experienced it first hand, and my feelings about it changed forever.

The music is a curiosity in that it's clearly folkloric, consisting at its most basic of accordion, rasp and drum, yet it's played everywhere, and it's the music that couples are most likely to get close and slow dance to, at least on the coast.

If it's everywhere on the coast, it's even more

everywhere during the festival, and that's best time to experience it. There are little bands playing everywhere you go — in supermarkets, shopping malls, back yards and so on — as well as stadium-scale concerts. There is even a competitive element: you can see the contest for the best accordion player, for example, and also *piquerías*, which are essentially rap battles for *vallenato* stars. Even if you're not so much a fan of the music, and more a fan of drinking large quantities of rum, then you'll enjoy it — a key part of the festival for many is glugging the night away in *parrandas* (private *vallenato* all-nighters).

You don't have to wait for the festival, either — live music in the city is commonplace. And, if you really get into it, there are music schools where you can go to learn to play it for yourself. So grasp the nettle — spend a little time in Valledupar — and you may find it grows on you after all. Or maybe not. Maybe you'll dislike it even more. But at least you'll have had good fun developing that antipathy.

7 — Lose all sense of time in Mompós

For many, Cartagena is the colonial jewel in this part of the country, but if you fancy something a little less pristine and tourist-thronged, then head inland to Mompós. Where Cartagena has an immaculately restored historic centre with a Benetton store, a Hard Rock Cafe and people trying to sell you stuff on every corner, Mompós is a quiet town of faded grandeur with an atmosphere all of its own.

Please excuse me for quoting once again from Dancing Feat:

"Trapped in a swampy lowland, where the Cauca and Magdalena rivers converge, the pace of life in Mompós is a step down from the coast, even. Folk sit out in front of their houses on rocking chairs, giving me friendly smiles as I pass, whilst cats roll out and stretch behind window grills. Colonial buildings bake in the midday sun and the corners of concrete sidewalks slowly disintegrate into the road. Green paint peels off a door in a decades-long process, revealing the previous coat, also green. Time doesn't flow here — it oozes."

Mompós

Mompós (also known as Mompox, or even Santa Cruz de Mompox) was once a trade rival to Cartagena. But while Cartagena was the official trade hub, Mompós was the centre for contraband.

There's not much to see here per se, but then to

come to see something would be to miss the point. For this is a place to come and hang out; to sit and eat a plate of fish with rice and plantain on the backwater river bank; to wonder how on earth you're going to develop the motivation to leave. The latter will definitely take some planning — perhaps a little nap first will help.

Getting to Mompós can be a little tricky, especially if you don't like early starts — the direct bus from Cartagena was leaving at 6:30am at the time of writing — but doing it in legs, via Magangué, can be fun and a mini-adventure in its own right. Check out the website of guest house La Casa Amarilla (http://bit.ly/1MVo2Vs) for more details and more options. In fact, check out La Casa Amarilla in general — I found it a splendid place to stay, and, if you're lucky, owner and journalist Richard McColl might be about. Few people are as well-informed about Colombia as Richard is, and it's also well worth checking out his podcast, Colombia Calling.

8 — Pedal the strip in Tolú

Tolú is a seaside town on the Caribbean coast. It's not a place to go and see old colonial architecture or that kind of thing. Rather, it's a place to go and see Colombians having a whole lot of fun – especially during holiday periods – and, with a bit of luck, to join them.

During the day, the activities in Tolú centre on larking about in the water on giant inflatables and/or taking day trips out to the San Bernardo Islands, but during the night, it's all about the *malecón* (promenade). On one side of the promenade are the bars and handicraft stalls, on the other, the dark void of the Caribbean Sea. In between the two is a flurry of over-sized pedal cars, with lights flashing and music blaring out.

The pedal cars are for hire — you provide the leg power and choose the music, and the driver (well, steerer) guides the vehicle up and down the *malecón*. It's like that whole 'cruising the strip' thing, only with the resulting street credibility somewhat compromised by the fact that you're all pedalling.

Minibuses to Tolú from Cartagena take about 3 hours. And, no — you're not expected to pedal.

9 — Walk the walls of Cartagena

The main entrance to historic Cartagena is a big old clock tower with arches underneath. Or maybe it's not: maybe it's the angular, salt-weathered wall that forms the perimeter — it probably depends on whether or not you're a colonial-era invading force. The wall's mere existence hints at the city's past as a place of great strategic importance to the Spanish, especially as a trading hub, and one which was subjected to attack on many occasions.

The wall itself is a big, fat, 'you ain't coming in' kind of construction that describes an irregular line around the outside of the historic centre. It's punctuated by regular cannons and there's a cafe-bar in one corner. Up top, it's plenty wide enough to walk along, with wooden bridges joining together the disparate sections. There's a faint smell of salt, and at certain times of the year you also get the warm blustery breeze of the Levante wind for company. It certainly makes a welcome escape from the heat and the hassle of the streets below.

Atop the wall at Cartagena

On one side of the wall are the city's cobbled streets and the clatter of horses and carriages. On the other, the Caribbean Sea glints in the sunlight and local fishermen try their luck with hand-held lengths of nylon. It's a particularly good place to see day turn to night, especially from the corner where the café is situated as across from here is the dog-leg peninsular of Bocagrande, whose high-rise apartments provide the perfect contrast with the old walls. You can sip a cocktail and watch as the sky turns pink, then darkens, and the lights come on one by one, the atmosphere of the city changing entirely in the process.

10 — Escape the heat in Minca

Even the locals can find the heat of the coast too much to bear at times, and Santa Marta in particular can get furiously hot. Fortunately, in the same way that every evil space tyrant has an escape pod, every hot Colombian city has some kind of cooling-down spot nearby. In the case of Santa Marta, this means the hillside retreat of Minca in the Sierra Nevada de Santa Marta mountains.

Nestling in the foothills of this, the world's highest coastal range, Minca is only half-an-hour away in time, yet it feels like a world away in other terms. Suddenly the air is breathable and the temperature has dropped a few notches.

As with seemingly every single touristic village in Latin America, you can hike to a series of waterfalls. The track in this particular example has the added attraction of an artfully collapsing bridge, and the wine-like scent from the fermenting fruits and berries that have fallen to the floor. As well as walking, you can also visit a coffee farm and a bird reserve. But in reality the main things to do here are relax, soak up the artistic atmosphere and enjoy the fact that you are no longer sweating profusely.

Getting to Minca usually involves taking a *colectivo* (share-taxi) up the road of twists, turns and failing asphalt. Or you could just pay the extra and take a private-hire taxi. There are more detailed instructions at the websites of Casa Loma Minca (http://casalomaminca.com) and Casa Elemento (http://www.casaelemento.com).

11 — Laze in a hammock at Tayrona National Park

A homage to sandy, palm-fringed beaches, Tayrona National Park is the single most-visited national park on mainland Colombia.

The coastline here consists of a string of boulder-strewn beaches, many of which choose crashing waves and dangerous currents over shore-lapping serenity. Vendors serve chargrilled fish with coconut rice from beach-side barbecues while visitors lie spread-eagled soaking up the rays, presumably as a knowing reference to the sun-worshipping Muisca people that shared a language with the indigenous Taironas.

Linking the beaches is a network of tracks that burrows into the coast's jungly interior, past the nesting sites of blue land-crabs, and you can also trek inland to the archaeological site of El Pueblito, which is like a mini-Ciudad Perdida (see #5). You can stay overnight, too, with accommodation ranging from simple hammocks to luxury cabañas.

There are various ways of getting to Tayrona National Park, including taking a bus from Santa Marta, or a taxi or boat from Taganga. Do be aware, though, that this is a national park, so there's an entrance fee and park rules apply. My own first attempt to go there was with a friend who was carrying pretty much just a speargun, but this was stymied when the taxi driver explained what you should and shouldn't be taking into a national park, the answers being a passport and a speargun respectively.

Tayrona National Park

12 — Go car-free at Capurganá

Once upon a time, Colombia and Panama were part of the same country — Gran Colombia — but in 1903 they separated amid politicking over the Panama Canal. As it is, the two countries — and indeed Central and South America — are separated not only by a border, but also by a largely impassable area known as the Darien Gap. This is a jungle-swathed region of extreme biodiversity, but also extreme danger due to the presence of various actors in the Colombian internal conflict. Even the Pan-American Highway takes a break at this point.

But there is one destination in this out-of-the-way area which you can get to quite reasonably, and that's the coastal village of Capurganá. Being right on the edge of the border in an area of prime rainforest, there is something missing — the constant rumble of traffic. Capurganá is so far out of the way that it's not even connected by road to the rest of the country.

Aside from the lack of cars and the white-sand beaches, the other interesting thing about this place is that it offers an alternative route into Panama. Small boats called *chalupas* go from here to Panama's Puerto Obaldia, though the latter is itself pretty isolated and has no onward road, so you would have to continue your journey by plane or possibly a merchant ship. This is definitely one to research thoroughly in advance, especially as regards cross-border immigration issues, and one to take extra care with safety-wise given the remote nature of these places.

As with a number of other villages along this coast, you can only get to Capurganá by boat, which you can do from Turbo (itself not exactly a major tourist hub). If you're simply looking to transit between Colombia and Panama, then a simpler option is a private yacht trip from Cartagena. The cost at the time of writing was in the region of US$400-500 for what is typically a 4-5 day journey including a 2-day layoff in Panama's idyllic San Blas islands. This is another one worth checking out ahead of time, as boats can get booked up well in advance.

13 — Fill up on backpacker culture in Taganga

Taganga is Colombia's gringo hangout *du jour* (no, I don't know why I'm speaking French, either). It made the mistake of being an idyllic village only 10-minutes' bus ride from Santa Marta, and hiding behind a big hill wasn't enough to save it.

If you tend to come away from home to be with people who are very similar to you but happen to be wearing flip-flops, then you'll absolutely adore this place. If, on the other hand, your flesh goes bumpy at the mere thought of other backpackers, then you might want to head elsewhere. Or at least stock up on anti-allergy pills.

For everyone else, it's just a pretty cool place to hang out for a few days and listen to the gentle fluttering of palms intermingling with chatter in multiple foreign languages. Chatter which is mostly about beaches, although occasionally about whether Ciudad Perdida is 'worth it', and how the steak in La Casa de Felipe is excellent (which it is). Taganga is also a good place to use as a base if you plan to do the Ciudad Perdida trek and/or visit Tayrona National Park.

14 — Laze in surreal surroundings at Cabo de la Vela

Cabo de la Vela, meaning the Cape of Sails, is a dramatic thumb of land in the remote and desertified La Guajira region of north-eastern Colombia. To say that this part of the world is where the sand meets the sea would be something of an understatement. It's where an entire desert meets the sea, *tierra firma* ending abruptly with the blue-green of the Caribbean.

The area is inhabited by the fiercely independent Wayuu people, who were famously never subjugated by the Spanish, but who are just about warming to the modern-day tourist invasion. I still wouldn't recommend riding up the beach on a horse demanding their compliance, though.

The fishing village adjoining the headland is a dusty place with an end of the world feel, the inhabitants mostly living in huts made from cactus. From here there are good walks out to beaches and a lighthouse, as well as the viewpoint of Pilón de Azucar. There's also the nearby Laguna de Utta, which is great for seasonal water birds. Or you could just chill on the beach, or in a hammock, as is common here.

If Cabo de la Vela is still not out-of-the-way enough, you can head for Punta Gallinas, an even more remote, more beautiful place that also happens to be the northernmost tip of South America.

Riohacha, the capital of La Guajira department, is a good jumping-off point for getting to Cabo de la Vela, but the journey is not exactly straightforward, generally requiring the use of a couple of separate *colectivos* (share taxis). Alternatively, you could go with a tour company from Santa Marta. Note that although plenty of independent travellers and tour groups regularly make it out to this spot, it's a region that has been unsafe for tourism at times, so seek advice before travelling.

15 — Plumb the depths of the Caribbean Sea

The Rosario and San Bernardo Corals National Park is Colombia's most-visited national park, with over 300,000 visitors per year. It's also not a 'park' in the traditional sense, being almost entirely underwater. Although perhaps, given the common use of garden comparisons when describing coral reefs, it actually is.

It's great a place for snorkelling, diving and even canoeing, or you could stuff the aquatics altogether and just admire the white-sand beaches of the national park via your back and a towel.

Tours to the Islas Rosarios depart from Cartagena, heading to Playa Blanca en route, which is the perfect spot if you like people trying to sell you things in beautiful surroundings. The San Bernardo Islands, which many consider superior, are more normally accessed from Tolú, some way further along the coast (see #8). You can read more about the national park at the colombia.travel website (http://www.colombia.travel/).

16 — Go whale watching on the Pacific Coast

The Caribbean side of Colombia is very well known to the country's visitors, but the Pacific side much less so. But as well as offering up that favourite the world over — the opportunity to lie down on hot sand — the Pacific Coast offers visitors something pretty special. And that's the chance to see whales.

Between mid-June and mid-October, migrating humpback whales and their young can be seen clearly from the shore at Bahía Solano. Alternatively, you can take a tour and get a bit closer. Obviously, this is not like some special show where the whales get paid to turn up, so it's worth checking the situation in advance of travelling, especially if you plan to visit on the fringes of the migration period.

The whole area is pretty remote and hard to access by land, on top of which there are security issues, so the best route in at the time of writing is by plane. But once you're out here, there are various other places to visit, such as the coastal town of Nuquí.

And whale-watching is not the only reason to visit this part of the country. The jungly Chocó region, populated mainly by people of African descent, has its own unique atmosphere and culture.

Do note that there are some real no-go areas on the Pacific Coast at the time of writing, so seek advice before travelling.

17 — Experience indigenous culture at Nabusimake

Despite the various trials that the indigenous peoples of Colombia have been subjected to over the past 500 years or so — subjugation and slavery, foreign diseases, the civil war and so on — there are still 83 recognised groups spread throughout the land. One such group is the Arhuaco people, who you can occasionally see around and about in Valledupar, dressed in white tunics, with sleek black hair and knitted beanies, and perhaps a woven bag.

The village of Nabusimake is effectively the Arhuaco capital. Set amidst the green splendour of the lower eaves of the Sierra Nevada de Santa Marta mountains, it's a settlement of *bahareque* (wattle and daub) houses with thatched roofs.

The Arhuaco people are extremely protective of their culture (and arguably any other stance would have seen them wiped out long ago). In general, they can be quite distant and disengaged from outsiders, as is their prerogative, so don't be offended if your attempts to engage meet with disinterest. Their village is certainly open to respectful visitors, though — something for which you must register and pay a small charge.

Nabusimake is not an easy place to get to, being some three hours up an unpaved road from the nearest town — something which arguably helps to protect it. There is no formal accommodation here, either, though you may be able to arrange for somewhere to stay through, for example, Provincia Hostel in Valledupar, who tend to be very helpful and informative in general. If you do go, then be respectful and don't point your camera where it isn't wanted. It's probably not a good idea to try and hold a stag / bachelor party here, either.

Valledupar (see also #6) is a good starting point to get to this isolated settlement. From there, take a *colectivo* to Pueblo Bello, and then another onwards, or take the daily bus. Try not to miss the return bus as it's a 38-kilometre walk back.

THE MOUNTAINOUS INTERIOR

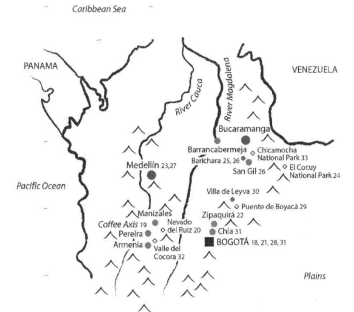

Caribbean Sea

PANAMA

VENEZUELA

River Cauca

River Magdalena

Bucaramanga

Barrancabermeja ◇ Chicamocha
Barichara 25, 26 National Park 33
San Gil 26 ◇ El Cocuy
National Park 24

Medellín 23,27

Pacific Ocean

Villa de Leyva 30

◇ Puente de Boyacá 29

Zipaquirá 22

Manizales

Coffee Axis 19   Nevado
Pereira ◇ del Ruiz 20   Chía 31
Armenia   Valle del   BOGOTÁ 18, 21, 28, 31
Cocora 32

Plains

18 — Gaze across the capital from Cerro de Monserrate

Colombia's capital, Bogotá, is home to about eight million residents, and it can be hard to get a sense of the place when you're down at street level, which is just one of the reasons to head up to the peak of Cerro de Monserrate.

Bogotá from Cerro de Monseratte

The city lies on a high-altitude plateau called the Sabana de Bogotá, but snuggles up to the adjacent green-clad mountains, and this is where Cerro de Monserrate is located. It's not just a viewpoint but a destination in its own right — there are a couple of restaurants, a church and a winding street of souvenir stalls. Both daytime and evening are good times to be here, and you can take the cable-car or the funicular railway to the top (or take one up and the other down).

Unfortunately, like many 'climb the hill adjacent to the city'-type attractions in Colombia, the path up the hillside can be something of a free-enterprise zone for thieves. So if you want to go on foot, then pick a time when there will be plenty of other people around, with Saturday or Sunday mornings generally being good times.

19 — Stay in a hacienda in the Coffee Axis

Colombia produces some excellent coffee, generally of the mild Arabica variety. Indeed, it has historically been one of the country's main exports. However, competition amongst coffee-growing countries has proliferated in recent years, meaning that exporting coffee isn't as profitable as it once was. As a result, many of the plantations in the Eje Cafetero (Coffee-growing axis) have opened themselves to agrotourism in order to supplement their income. This is great for visitors as it means the chance to stay at a functioning *hacienda* in the heart of the combed hillsides, for instance at Hacienda Guayabal (http://www.haciendaguayabal.com/) or at Hacienda Venecia (http://www.haciendavenecia.com/).

At such haciendas, you get a chance to walk the plantation and see the whole process of coffee production, from the growing of fledgling plants in the nursery to the roasting and grinding of the harvested beans. You'll see how they separate the low-grade stuff that ends up as *tinto*, sold from vacuum flasks in every square in Colombia, from the high-grade export product, which many Colombians unfortunately never get to taste. And finally you'll get a chance to taste a fresh cup, made right there and then.

So if you like spending your days with a fixed stare, but want to stay on the right side of the law, then this is the place to come. The main cities in the area, and hence good jumping-off points, are the triumvirate of Manizales, Armenia and Pereira.

The Coffee Axis

20 — Climb Nevado del Ruiz

If you like the idea of conquering a volcano by the adventurous method of driving a vehicle nearly all of the way up it, then Nevado del Ruiz is the place to go.

The approach by road itself is quite something. The scenery first changes to *páramo* — high altitude tree-less scrub, and a place where you can see the rare *frailejón* plant — and then again to an ashen pumice, devoid of all vegetation. The effects of the altitude quickly become evident, too — I went up there with some fellow travellers in a hire car, and even the engine was struggling to catch its breath as we neared the start point of the hiking trail.

The trek is from 4,800m to 5,100m above sea-level. But whilst a 300m ascent might not seem like much of a challenge, the altitude makes it a completely different prospect. It's a long slow drudge, and even just going at the gentlest pace is hugely consuming — you'll almost certainly have no breath left over for conversation. And even if the lack of oxygen doesn't defeat you, the weather might — our (obligatory) guide called our ascent to a disappointing halt to at 5,000m as the mist and rain had made the path too slippery, and hence too dangerous. Not that anyone complained.

Nevado del Ruiz is near the city of Manizales and can be visited as part of a tour, or independently with a hire car. Come well prepared, as it can get very cold, and be sure you're aware of and prepared for the health implications of being at high altitude. Also note that this is an active volcano — it erupted with tragic consequences in 1985, killing around 23,000 people.

21 — Ride a steam train out of Bogotá

There are very few opportunities to take the train in Colombia, or indeed in South America in general, which is a shame given its rich heritage of banditry. However there is still the occasional chance to partake, and one of those is on the steam train that runs out of Bogotá. This is an experience not to be missed, given that it allows you to combine the novelty of Colombian train travel with that of having a soot-coated face should you stick your head out the window at the wrong moment. Something which, of course, is a really bad idea at the best of times.

Many people use this train service as a way to get to the salt mines at Zipaquirá (see #22), but it's actually a more than worthwhile activity in its own right. You get to see something of the Sabana de Bogotá (the grassy plateau in the Andes on which the city resides), and also to spend time in the company of Bogotanos relaxing and having fun.

During the journey, bands of musicians pass through the carriages playing typical music, with passengers calling out or clapping along in time. No sooner will one band have departed then another will arrive playing an entirely different genre, giving you the chance to experience everything from the accordion-based vallenato of the coast to the panpipe music of the Andes, all without leaving your seat. Food and drink vendors also squeeze by, selling coffee in plastic cups, *tamales* (pork and maize wrapped up in a plantain leaf) and other things besides.

The whole time, the train sashays along to its own rhythm: the chattering of wheels on the track, the ringing of bells at level crossings and the occasional shriek of someone spilling hot coffee on themselves due to the movement of the carriage.

The service generally only runs on weekends and public holidays, and at the time of writing the round trip in high season cost 59,000 COP (about US$20). For more information, including how to book, go to the Turistren website (http://www.turistren.com.co/).

22 — Visit a salt cathedral in Zipaquirá

If the term 'salt cathedral' summons up the image of a free-standing cathedral built from salt, with a spire and buttresses, then you need to knock that down and start again — the reality is the inverse of that.

Inside the salt mine at Zipaquirá

Burrowed into a hillside above the town of Zipaquirá is an industrial-scale salt mine and, within that, chambers have been hollowed out to form the insides of a cathedral, with an apse, wooden seating and echoey acoustics to boot. And this is not some scratchy little affair, either — it's a vast network of man-made caverns and interconnecting tunnels.

Descending into the broad-bore tunnel, the natural light all soon disappears, replaced by a rich smell of sulphur. On your way down, you pass the various 'stations of the cross' — big stone crosses set in their own caverns — before eventually arriving at the unfeasibly large chambers. The lighting — all eery greens and prophetic blues — gives the place an atmosphere, as does the dripping ceiling, which also provides the free souvenir of a saline-encrusted scalp.

A good way of getting to the salt mines is on an excursion from Bogotá. If the timing is right, you could take the steam train out there and make a whole day of it (see #21).

23 — Ride the *metrocable* up out of Medellín

Colombia has changed a lot in recent times, but probably nowhere has had quite as dramatic a transformation as Medellín. Indeed, until fairly recently, this place was to be avoided. It was the country's most murderous city in the world's most murderous country; the former epicentre of drugs, assassinations and kidnapping, and the erstwhile home of Pablo Escobar. In short, it was the home of everything that Colombia was infamous for.

But nowadays it's a place that attracts high numbers of visitors, not least due to its spring-like climate and its reputation for beautiful women, the latter making it a particularly good place to go if you like watching foreign men practising their pick-up techniques. It has also become a destination popular with digital nomads.

The city's renaissance was due in part to the construction of the *metrocable*, a public-transport cable-car system which, along with a modern overhead railway, allowed areas of the city that were deprived and isolated to be pulled into a tighter embrace with the rest of the city, thus stopping the poor from being marginalised quite so much in ghettos.

As a visitor you can use it to enjoy the breathtaking views as it climbs out of the Aburrá Valley. But it's also a serious piece of public transport — around 30,000 people use it on a daily basis.

You can read more about it on the Metro de Medellín website (http://bit.ly/1A3DYKX).

24 — Hike snowy peaks in El Cocuy National Park

You may have noticed this already, but Colombia is kind of mountainous. This torn-up terrain, which historically made travel and trade so difficult, is also a major part of the country's appeal, and a source of great beauty. If only there was some way of interacting with this natural splendour…

El Cocuy National Park, in the Andes' Cordillera Oriental, contains a magnificent collection of snow-capped peaks — there are 15 of 5,000 metres and above — with great opportunities for hiking. You get to experience the Colombian *páramo* (which means plenty of *frailejónes* — see also #20), plus waterfalls, lakes and wildlife. Oh, and mountains. You'll see plenty of mountains.

There are two conveniently-situated villages from which to strike out. Güicán, a 12-hour direct coach journey from Bogotá, is the more popular for starting hikes, but El Cocuy is generally considered the more attractive settlement. There are plenty of day hikes, or you can do the main circuit between Güicán and El Cocuy in about six or seven days. You don't even have to hike at all — if it suits you, you can just hang around in one of the villages and point at the nice landscape.

Guides and horses are available for hire. Maybe some of the horses double as guides — I don't know. I do know, however, that you need to come well equipped, and to make sure you understand the implications of the effects of altitude.

25 — Walk between beautiful villages in Santander

Set amongst the peaks and gorges of the eastern cordillera of the Andes, the department of Santander is a very special part of the country. And as if the landscape weren't enough, it's also host to a number of beautiful colonial villages, which lie scattered like breadcrumbs amidst its ruffled-tablecloth scenery. One such village is Barichara, and another is nearby Guane, the latter being arguably just a hamlet. With the two places being linked by an old *camino de herradura* (bridlepath), you can easily visit the two in a day, hiking between them.

Barichara, a 45-minute bus ride from San Gil, is a quiet village of white-washed houses and stone-laid streets, and must be amongst the most beautiful villages in all of Colombia. It's also situated on a hillside, so when you get bored of sitting in the quiet leafy gardens, with birds swooping down from trees all about you, there's a canyon to go and gawp at.

Andean skies at Barichara

Guane somehow manages to be a step down activity-wise even from this. On my own visit there, I only saw two cars, and they were both parked. Effectively, there was no traffic at all aside from the human kind. Local people wandered about, occasionally joining each other for a chat. Others sat out on benches or the sidewalk, else hung about in each other's shops. That seemed to be pretty much all there was to do. A farmer out working in the nearby field was the nearest thing I saw to heavy industry. A wander up a hill led me up to what must be one of the world's most scenic cemeteries, the various headstones and crosses resting peacefully against a backdrop of serious mountainside.

The old path joining the two villages is fittingly quiet, and feels like a step back in time. Rebuilt from the original, it's paved all the way with hefty stones and meanders along the canyon-side, guiding the walker under tree canopies and past cactii. You can get from Barichara to Guane in something like an hour and a half, or maybe two, depending on how much you dawdle.

From Guane, a bus eventually heads back to San Gil. If it can be bothered.

26 — Eat fat-bottomed ants in San Gil

Hormigas culonas or fat-bottomed ants (the Queen song that never was) are one of Colombia's — and Santander Department's — most famed regional specialities. You can buy them in plastic cups on the street, or in corner shops, in places like San Gil and other towns and villages thereabouts.

On my own trip, I went for a more culinary option, at the unfortunately since-closed Color de Hormiga restaurant in Barichara, where they integrated them into their menu. When the dish arrived it took me a few moments to work out what I was looking at — surely those big blobs on the chicken breast weren't the ants? Oh yes they were. There were no legs or mandibles — or whatever it is ants have — and unlike many of the ants one encounters in Colombia, they weren't carrying bits of leaf. Which was perhaps a missed opportunity —

it would certainly have been a novel way of introducing sage or tarragon to the dish.

A squadron of fat-bottomed ants in Barichara

So what did it taste like? Well, at the risk of reinforcing stereotypes, for me it tasted like chicken. Because that's what I ordered. But with the accompanying crunching sound of ants. The flavour was quite subtle: coffee-like, maybe even slightly chocolaty, but also nutty. Perhaps also a bit like an ashtray.

One problem with eating something like ant is that it's very hard to actually enjoy it. Even if the flavour were exquisite, you'd still be thinking "Wait a minute — I'm eating ant!" every few seconds. But if you like the odd culinary adventure to accompany your wanderings, and have the child-like propensity to put things in your mouth that generally belong on the floor, then it's worth trying out.

27 — Pose with Botero's plump statues in Medellín

Despite Medellín's reputation for attractive women, not everyone there meets societal norms, of anatomical perfection. Indeed, parts of the centre are inhabited by hugely oversized people — individuals with trunk-like necks, thunderous buttocks and fingers that just about manage to taper down enough to look vaguely useable.

These are the sculptures of the renowned, Medellín-born artist Fernando Botero. Everything he touches turns to fat – not overspilling fat, but something taut-skinned, pert and cheeky – with animals, people and inanimate objects being plumped up to the point where conventional proportion is forgotten.

Twenty-three of his works can be found in the Plaza de las Esculturas (aka Botero Plaza), and more still can be found in other parts of Medellín and, indeed, other parts of the country. There's a reclining nude in the historic centre of Cartagena, for instance, and there are both paintings and sculptures in the Museo Botero del Banco de la Republica in Bogotá. Some of his sculptures have even wandered as far as Armenia. And by that I do mean the country, rather than the Colombian city of the same name.

28 — Sate your gold lust in Bogotá

The hunt for gold was one of the main driving factors in the Spanish exploration of South America. And gold was certainly present in that part of the world — the indigenous people fashioned it into exquisite ornaments, though its value was as something sacred and tribal rather than monetary. Once the Spanish arrived, they began mining it with slaves, and even required that the indigenous people paid part of their *encomienda* (obligatory tribute to their colonial overlords) in it.

But such is the lure of the lustrous yellow stuff, and the greed it inspires, that merely taking all the gold that was available was never going to be enough. Cue the legend of El Dorado — the mythical City of Gold. In actual fact, El Dorado wasn't a place at all, but a chief of the Muisca people who, as an initiation rite, would be covered in gold dust and go out on a raft onto Lake Guatavita. But a combination of imagination, story-telling and wild-eyed desire meant that the name became associated with a presumed hidden empire of gold that it was thought the chief must preside over. Over the years, various expeditions were launched for it, and men died trying to find it, presumably never having read or watched The Treasure of the Sierra Madre with its fairly clear lessons on avarice.

If it's real, non-mythical gold that interests you, magnificent examples of pre-Columbian ornaments can be seen in Bogotá's Museo del Oro (Gold Museum). It's an astonishing place, featuring figurines, ceremonial masks and many other items, crafted by methods such as moulding (via the 'lost wax' method) and flattening (via the 'belting it with a hammer' method). The standout piece — found in a ceramic pot, in a cave, in 1969 — is an intricate golden raft (high bling factor, poor floatability), representing the aforementioned scene on

Lake Guatavita with El Dorado ('The Golden One').

There are other gold museums around the country — in Santa Marta, for instance — and you can also take a day trip from Bogotá to Lake Guatavita itself.

The Muisca raft in the Gold Museum, Bogotá

29 — Soak up some history at Puente de Boyacá

Puente de Boyacá holds a special place in Colombian history — it's the place where Símon Bolívar and his troops won a famous victory in the battle which definitively won the war of independence. If you're quietly thinking 'Who is Símon Bolívar?' then he was El Libertador (The Liberator) — a military and political figure who played a huge role in liberating Latin America — and South America in particular — from Spain. The country of Bolivia and the Venezuelan currency are both named after him, as are numerous towns and departments in various countries in South America, Colombia included. Statues of the great man march across the continent to this day.

The site is located in Colombia's mountainous heartlands, where locals wearing *ruanas* (heavy woollen ponchos) work the misty hillsides, and where the land is divided into many small farms. It consists of statues and columns, a special flame that never goes out (they should read up on the triangle of combustion — they'll have that sorted in no time) and coach-loads of Colombian visitors. They've since cleaned up all the dead bodies, which is always going to diminish the war-like atmosphere, and the bridge, which is the historical focal point, is surprisingly diminutive, but then it is symbolic of the formation of the nation, and that's no small thing.

Puente de Boyacá is a short hop by bus from Tunja, itself a 4-hour coach journey from Bogotá.

30 — Cross South America's biggest cobbled square at Villa de Leyva

Villa de Leyva is something you can get kind of used to in the Boyacá and Santander departments of Colombia — it's yet another stunning Andean town. Founded in the 16th century, it's all white-washed walls, red-tiled roofs and wooden balconies, the streets being cobbled with big, chunky stones.

As well as being pleasant to walk around, there are some good places to visit, too. Like the preserved period house of Antonio Nariño, who was a general in the fight for independence in the south of the country and also translated the Rights of Man from French to Spanish. Which is perhaps not so impressive in the era of Google Translate, but was probably quite a big deal back then.

The main square at Villa de Leyva

The real masterpiece, though, is the Plaza Mayor (Main Square), a large cobbled area which rolls like the hills surrounding the town. It's big — said to be the largest cobbled square in South America — and it feels even bigger just because of the time it takes to navigate the tricky surface. When I was there they were in the process of filling in the gaps between the huge cobbles with cement, presumably to reduce the need for a permanent St John's Ambulance service presence on standby in each corner.

As with Barichara and Guane (see #25), Villa de Leyva is set in sumptuous countryside, and is a good place to do some hiking, or to go exploring via bicycle or horseback.

31 — Fill your boots (and your stomach) in Bogotá

Colombian culinary staples have changed very little since colonial times, with rice, potatoes, corn, beans and plantain being the regulars in the cheap, ubiquitous lunch which forms the main meal of the day. It's usually cooked without herbs, spices or other seasonings, meaning that the flavours can be quite subtle. Indeed, many backpackers, with their well-travelled palates, can find themselves on a quest for more variety, especially those whose tongues are still singing from all the spices they've encountered on, say, a visit to Southeast Asia.

Fortunately, Bogotá is a great place to expand on that diet, and you definitely shouldn't leave without trying the wonderful local dish of Ajiaco.

Ajiaco, Bogotá-style, is a creamy chicken stew with potatoes, hunks of corn and the bite of capers. Yellow-green in colour with a swirl of cream on top, it's served with a side of avocado and rice, and has a heartiness that sets it aside from thinner Colombian stews such as the broth-like sancocho. There are a number of slightly touristy — but nonetheless great — places to try it in Bogotá's colonial district of La Candelaria. Specifically, head for Calle 11, just off the famous Plaza Bolivar — for example Mama Lupe (Calle 11 No. 6-14).

Another great option for food in Bogotá is the

legendary Andrés Carne de Res. This is primarily a steakhouse and seafood restaurant, but it also attempts to answer the question as to how many illuminated love-hearts and other lit-up paraphernalia can be successfully suspended from a single ceiling. The electricity bill alone must be horrendous, and it's the kind of place where you could have an epileptic fit even if you didn't suffer from the condition. But merely to call it kitsch or gaudy would be to do it a disservice, as it's a place that consumes your senses and simply throbs with the party spirit. Oh, and the food's good too. The original is in Chía, just outside of Bogotá, but there are also branches in Bogotá itself.

32 — Test your neck muscles in Valle de Cocora

There's a lot of wonderful scenery in Colombia's coffee zone, but the misty Valle de Cocora (Cocora Valley) stands out as being particularly special due to its being stocked with a plethora of 50 to 60-metre high wax-palm trees. The wax palm is Colombia's national tree, and the tallest variety of palm in the world.

Down in the valley, cows casually mooch about at the bottom of the slender giants, as though it's normal for a tree to be that tall and yet have no foliage or branches until the very top. The valley is great for hiking, and is best accessed from the splendid little town of Salento.

It's also worthwhile to spend some time in Salento itself. Here, locals hang about in hats and ponchos next to white-washed houses with brightly-painted *zócalos* (skirtings), whilst jeeps in an array of colours line up on the main square like dancing girls. The town has become a backpacker favourite, and is a good place to experience the coffee zone in general.

33 — Paraglide into the Chicamocha canyon

There are precious few occasions in life when jumping off a precipice into a massive gorge is a good idea, but one of those occasions might be if you're going paragliding in the Chicamocha Canyon. Of the many great vistas to be found in the Andes, this one, located on the main road between San Gil and Bucaramanga, is right up there with the best of them.

Chicamocha National Park

Nearby San Gil is a good place to base yourself for a visit, given it's the home of adventure sport in

Colombia, and at the time of writing Parapente Chicamocha (http://www.parapentechicamocha.com/) seems to be a good company to do it with according to users of tripadvisor (http://bit.ly/17TsT8M).

Those less-inclined to put their trust in aerodynamics, but still with a desire to gape open-mouthed into the abyss, can take the cable car across instead, or just stay up top on the 360-degree viewing deck.

THE PLAINS AND THE AMAZON

34 — Be mesmerised by *joropo* in Villavicencio

Every region of Colombia has its own tradition of music and dance, and the Llanos (the plains that cover a large portion of Colombia and neighbouring Venezuela) are no different.

Here the main genre is *joropo*, a partner-based dance whose movements contain plenty of nods to both the wildlife of the area and the cattle-farming industry. The footwork can represent everything from galloping horses to different types of birds, whilst the stance of the lead, typically the man in a male-female pairing, is like a cowboy driving cattle by its horns, whilst the manner in which he turns his partner is evocative of a lasso.

Far from being just an interesting dance in cultural terms, *joropo* in full flow can be a thrilling sight, especially when done by professionals. It's a fantastically difficult dance due to the fact that it incorporates so many elements, such as waltzing, elaborate turns and complex foot patterns. It's also one of the few dances that features an acoustic element — dancers wear special shoes called *cotizas* that allow them to spank the floor, setting sparks flying in the fast sections.

There are a couple of clubs in Villavicencio where you can witness people dancing *joropo*: El Botalón and Pentagrama Llano y Folclor. You can also ask at the tourist information office, and consider visiting the dance schools in Villavicencio and/or the neighbouring Acacías. If you're lucky, you might get to see a demonstration. The music alone is worth seeking out, as it has a beautiful lulling element to it, being primarily harp-based. You may be able to experience it being played live in one of the aforementioned clubs.

I spent a week learning *joropo* for the book Dancing Feat. It was amongst the hardest dances I learned and, whilst great fun, not particularly useful outside of the region, so I'd only recommend trying to do likewise if you have plenty of time to spare. And a general fondness of stamping.

35 — Stand in the centre of the country at Puerto López

If the geographical centre of the country was in the middle of a field, then that would be a little boring. Fortunately (and almost a little too conveniently) the dead centre happens to be located on the only hill in a very large radius, just outside the town of Puerto López.

From up on high, near the obelisk that marks the spot, you can see that the plains are really plain. It's like someone planed them with a giant plane, until they were so plain you could land one of those flying things on them. That's right — a helicopter.

The view here is a somewhat wilder and less-developed one than you get from the vantage points in the Andean hillsides such as at Villavicencio and Yopal — outwards stretch the fields, the trees, and the savannah, which, depending on the season, may or may not have a mirror of water on the surface.

I found it a good place to get a feel for the plains without getting too deep in, as many consider this larger territory somewhere you really shouldn't go "unless you're a bloody idiot" due to the presence of various actors in the civil war (by which I mean armed combatants, not re-enactment hobbyists). But, as always, you should still check for up-to-date information to make sure it's safe to go.

Buses run to Puerto López from Villavicencio. To get from the town to the hill you can take a taxi / auto-rickshaw.

Los Llanos, as seen from the obelisk at Puerto López

36 — Drink *agua de panela con queso* in Villavicencio

If you want to get a feel for the plains without actually having to go out into them, then this is the spot for you. The place in question is La Piedra del Amor (The Rock of Love) — a mountainside restaurant located where the Andes transition with surprising immediacy into the plains. Here you can gaze into the infinite and enjoy a cup of *agua de panela con queso* — a hot, sugar cane-based drink complete with dunking cheese, not unlike the *chocolate con queso* experience at Kilometro 18 (see #42).

Out there, somewhere beyond the horizon, are the mega-ranches, the capillary roads serving them and the wide-open spaces of the Llanos, much of which is generally a huge no-go area due to the internal conflict. To the northeast, the plains continue unabated to Venezuela, whilst to the southeast they coalesce into the Amazon rainforest. It's all something to rub your chin and ponder over as the sun drops behind the mountains and the lights begin to come on, defining all the little settlements and networks of roads that were previously hidden on the flat surface.

The town of Villavicencio is a couple of hours outside of Bogotá, and La Piedra del Amor is a quick taxi ride out of town and up the hillside.

37 — Catch the sunrise in Yopal

It would seem like the activity most associated with the plains is standing in an elevated position and admiring how flat they are. This is yet another variation on that theme.

Yopal is one of numerous towns on the plains that clings to the hem of the Andes. It's a small town, but it's clean and quite a lively place. It also appears to have a disproportionately large red-light district, perhaps for all the workers that come to town after months on the range and/or from the oil fields. The thing the place is best known for amongst Colombians, however, is not its evenings but its mornings. Specifically its sunrise.

Sunrise over the Llanos at Yopal

One of the best spots to see this famous sunrise is on the side of the encroaching Andes, at a spot by the statue of the Virgen de Manare, who is the patron of the plains folk.

Crosses and statues erected at high vantage points on a city's outskirts are a regular feature of Colombia. They're great for getting a view of the environs although the paths leading up to such places are often frequented by thieves and muggers, so beware, and only visit at popular times. Fortunately, this particular spot is generally well-frequented with joggers in the mornings, which is traditionally when you're likely to be there if you've gone to experience the sunrise.

On my own visit, I didn't get to see what all the fuss was about, as the weather wasn't great. The statue briefly glowed as dawn broke, but for the most part the sun's rays were diffused by a layer of mist and low clouds. It was still pretty darned pleasant, though.

You can get to Yopal by minibus from Villavicencio, on the road which runs along the apron where the plains meet the mountains, or by heading down out of the Andes from Sogamoso.

38 — Gape at the strange beauty of Caño Cristales

Caño Cristales is a river in Colombia's Meta department. It's sometimes known as El Río de los Cinco Colores (The River of Five Colours) and is also one of those must-be-seen-to-be-believed places that frequently appear on those internet lists of extraordinary sights.

The river comes off the huge tepui-like mesa of the Serranía de la Macarena, and appears to run red because of an aquatic plant that blooms during a specific time of the year. There are also circular pools in the river, along with other strange geological features.

It's neither cheap nor easy to get there, as you have to take a flight from Villavicencio or Bogotá. It's also in a region which has historically been problematic in terms of kidnapping, so (as with all travel in Colombia), you should seek up-to-date advice, although at the time of writing the British Government's FCO map suggested it was located in a little pocket of okay-ness (http://bit.ly/1uzGY3s). In terms of the river's colours, the best time is usually late July to November.

39 — Explore the Amazon at Leticia

In the southeast of the country is a peculiar zip tag of land — the result of a war with neighbouring Peru in the 1930s. And it's here that Colombia meets not only Peru but also Brazil, in a three-way coming together of nations. More importantly, at least from a doing-cool-stuff point of view, it's where Colombia meets the Amazon River, the latter forming part of the country's southern border.

If you've always wanted to stomp about in an exotic part of the world, scaring away some of the rarest and most beautiful species of wildlife known to man, then here's your chance. You can explore the jungle and the river, go bird watching, take part in night-time safaris and even leave Colombia altogether to explore a couple of other countries. Indeed, it's said that you can have breakfast in Colombia, lunch in Peru and dinner in Brazil, like some kind of food-obsessed, country-ticking show-off.

To explore Colombia's section of the Amazon, head to the town of Leticia, which is most usually accessed by plane from Bogotá.

THE SOUTH

40 — Learn to dance salsa in Cali

Cali lives and breathes salsa in a way very few other places in the world can lay claim to. Indeed, not only is Cali a good place to go if you want to dance salsa, it's actively a bad place to go if you want to avoid it. Seriously — if you end up on a night out with a group of Colombians, don't expect to be able to sit on the sidelines and watch. You'll practically need your leg in plaster to get away with not dancing here, and even that is by no means certain to work.

The link with salsa dates back to the time when Cali was an important trade hub, and sailors used to bring records in by the boxload from Cuba to the nearby port of Buenaventura, giving the city a link with the Caribbean and salsa's precursors.

There are various different types of salsa dancing around the world. Cali is home to its very own style, featuring fast and intricate footwork, and the city is full of clubs with people dancing it. Indeed many clubs are dedicated to salsa alone. Note that the city generally likes its salsa fast, as befits the dancing, and it has its own classic tracks, such as Cali Pachanguero by Grupo Niche and Oiga, Mire, Vea by Orquesta Guayacán.

If you want to dance salsa in Cali, don't expect to be able to just wing it. Even a knowledge of New York or LA-style salsa won't get you too far, as the style danced here is significantly different. Fortunately there are probably more dance schools in Cali than anywhere else in Colombia, so there is no shortage of options for learning afresh or adapting your existing style. Some schools offer group classes, but if you're only in town for a short period of time then it's best to take an intensive course of individual lessons.

The usefulness of Cali-style salsa outside of Colombia is fairly limited — New York, LA and Cuban style are all more-readily encountered globally — but as an introduction to partner dancing it's great. Plus going out dancing here is the best way to get an insider pass into what is a fundamental part of the city's culture. It's also good if you want to repeat the words, "*Uno, dos, tres … cinco, seis, siete,*" so often that you start saying them in your sleep.

I spent over month just in Cali, and the finale of my dance journey took place here. It's one of the natural homes of dance in a country that's obsessed with it.

If you want to know more on the subject, check out my brief guide — How to Learn to Dance in Colombia (http://amzn.com/B00ZIVDDV4). It contains all the stuff I wish I'd known before I went out there, including how to find a good school, dance etiquette, overcoming fear of the dance floor and so on.

41 — Go volcanic at Laguna Verde

There are lots of good hiking opportunities in Colombia, but the one to Laguna Verde is particularly special. It's actually a crater lake in the semi-dormant Azufral volcano, and can be done as a (long) day trip from Pasto.

The early part of the trek is across treeless *páramo* with the kind of strange, dense growths that prosper at such altitudes and in such perpetually moist air. From here, there are great views looking out over the open plains to the south — you may even be able to see as far as Ecuador if you're lucky — though on my own visit, visibility was pretty appalling for much of the time.

After reaching the high point, you descend a gritty path down into the crater. This is when the *laguna* comes into sight if the weather is favourable — beach-like shores encapsulating a tear-shaped, milky green body of water whose colour comes from deposits of sulphur and iron. There are a couple of other, smaller, lakes in there, too — Laguna Negra and Laguna Cristal.

If you ever have the chance to go hiking with Colombian friends, take it. I went up with a group of people from Pasto, and it was here that I had my own experience of Colombian sharing. I'd stocked up on provisions for myself — a pot of yoghurt, a chocolate bar and so on — only to discover that everybody else had deliberately bought multiple items that they could share out with the rest of the group, making me feel unfeasibly mean (which I am, but I'm just usually so much better at hiding it). Further than that, when the weather turned bad, a couple with a poncho between the two of them insisted on sharing this scant patch of fabric even further, the thing snapping in the wind as we all huddled together, penguin-like, underneath.

Visiting Laguna Verde as a day trip from Pasto necessitates an early start, as you first have to head out to the town of Túquerres. Once there, you then need to arrange 4x4 transport to the park entrance, as well as agreeing on a pick-up time for the return journey. A simpler alternative might be to go with a tour group from Pasto.

The hike is not a long one, but it's tough due to the

high altitude (around 4,000m at the summit). The weather can be very changeable, too, so go well-prepared.

Laguna Verde

42 — Drink *chocolate con queso* at Kilometro 18

Kilometro 18 is a place in the Andes named after how far up the road it is. The appeal of the place is that it offers a refreshing mountain chill to those who need to escape Cali's valley heat. So great can the temperature difference be that it's also a place where you can have the novelty of seeing Caleños — people for whom even a light jacket is a rarity — wearing hats, gloves and scarves.

To get there, take a hire car or taxi and head out on

Ruta Nacional 19, which winds up out of Cali and into the mountains. The focal point of Kilometro 18 is a spur off the main highway which is lined with little bars and cafés. From here you can see the city flowing into the irregular valley floor spaces below. Well, on a good day, at least. When I was there it was a misty night, and we couldn't see a thing except for the line of cars hustling for spaces, and some well wrapped-up vendors caramelising corn over grates.

The done thing up here is to snuggle up to a warming *chocolate con queso*: a mug of hot chocolate served with Jenga-like blocks of white cheese. Whilst this might sound kind of sickly, the combination works well because the cheese is fairly neutral in taste, and quite waxy. Even if the combination is not one that makes you salivate, it's still a great opportunity to make a complete mess of the tablecloth, as you drop the depth charge-like blocks of cheese into the chocolatey deep of your drink.

43 — Experience an Andean market at Silvia

On market day, indigenous Guambiano people from the various villages in the area come to buy and sell produce in the little Andean town of Silvia. The climate is chilly, but they're suitably attired to cope, the women sporting royal blue shawls and the men wearing bright pink, or sometimes purple, wrap-around skirts. They complete the outfit with hefty walking boots and a hat halfway between a bowler and a fedora atop their dark hair.

Out in the streets, grunting old *chivas* — brightly-coloured, open-sided rural buses — shuttle locals in and out of town, their roofs loaded high with goods. The indoor market, meanwhile, resonates with the thud and clatter of potatoes hitting scales and people talking prices, a cafe in the corner sending out steamy invites from its bubbling stock pots.

Geometric designs at Silvia

Pretty much everything you need for life in the Andes is here: huge pots and pans, massive sacks of rice, and vegetables that are as irregular and lumpy as nature intended, plus machetes, pigs heads on hooks, hats and the bright yarns that go into making the many colourful fabrics you'll see worn around town.

Silvia is an easy day trip from Popayán. If you want to experience the market, then it's probably a good idea to go on market day, which at last check was Tuesday.

44 — Chill out at Laguna de la Cocha

Just outside of Pasto is a little village that feels curiously misplaced. Nestling on the inlet to a big lake — Laguna de la Cocha — it's a little settlement of colourful clapboard houses, reed beds and cute bridges.

Wooden boats sit on the channel, making it feel strangely reminiscent of a European canal town. It's certainly like nowhere else I've seen in Colombia. *Ruana*-wearing locals push bicycles about, whilst cats sit on window ledges watching nothing happen, which it does a lot.

Clapboard houses at Laguna de la Cocha

It's a lovely place just to hang out, eat fresh trout and maybe take a boat out to the nearby island, which has a nature walk where the trees are festooned with bromelia.

On my own visit there, the village calm was diminished somewhat by the sound of a squealing pig. It turned out that this was because it was being slaughtered, an event to put a frown on the faces of most creatures. They've probably finished with it by now, though, so I wouldn't let that put you off.

You can get to Laguna de la Cocha by *colectivo* (share taxi) from Pasto.

45 — Discover pre-Columbian wonders at San Agustín

If you like trekking or horse-riding amongst ancient stone statues — or if you don't know whether you do or not, but are interested in finding out — then this the place for you. There are more than 500 statues scattered in the hillsides of this UNESCO World Heritage Site, nestling between the Cauca and Magdalena valleys. Even if you're not into the whole stroking-your-chin-in-the-presence-of-pre-Columbian-stonework thing, this is still a good place to come simply to explore the beautiful surroundings.

An alternative in a similar vein is Tierradentro, which retains the beautiful mountain scenery but swaps statues for tombs.

If you're not sure whether you're a statue person or a tomb person (a dichotomy most of us have probably wrestled with at some point) you can find out more about about San Agustín and Tierradentro at the UNESCO website (http://bit.ly/17uFn6X).

Popayán makes a good jumping off point to go to see

either, whilst the town of Pitalito is the conduit to get between one and the other, though be aware that public transport is pretty limited in that regard. Note also that the whole area in which the two sites are located has been guerrilla territory in the past so, as always, make sure you're up to date with the current situation.

46 — Take sanctuary in a chasm at Ipiales

Deep in the south of Colombia, as the country is taking its last few breaths before magically transforming into Ecuador, it presents visitors with one last gift: El Sanctuario de Las Lajas.

Near the border town of Ipiales is a chasm, and it's within this chasm that you'll find the Sanctuario — a neo-Gothic structure which is a combination of church and bridge, and which spans the divide between the two steep, vegetation-soaked hillsides. The significance of the location is the apparent sighting of an apparition of the Virgin Mary in 1754. Just for added effect, the Guáitara River storms between the columns below.

You can admire the edifice from on high (by stopping at the viewpoint above the gorge, en route), at eye-level (by mooching about on the bridge itself) or down low (by taking the path down to the chasm floor). It's worth going inside the church too, even if you're not on a pilgrimage, as the back wall is formed by a rock face, making for an intriguing sight.

To get there, head for the bus station at Ipiales, where *colectivos* (share taxis) run to the site of the sanctuary.

47 — Explore badlands in the Tatacoa Desert

If you've never been to badlands before, they're not as malevolent as they sound. In fact they're really kind of cool. Due to a geological phenomenon involving sedimentary rock and exposure to the elements, the land in such places has become selectively eroded, creating all sorts of ravines and gullies, often in multiple colours. The outcome can be stunning to look at and maze-like to navigate.

Tatacoa Desert

Here in Colombia, not far from the town of Neiva, is an area of badlands called the Desierto de Tatacoa (Tatacoa Desert), which is easily accessible by visitors and which makes for a very worthwhile experience.

To really appreciate this area, and to avoid getting lost and dying, you should take a tour with an experienced local guide who'll lead you along dried-up watercourses and through winding ravines. It's slow going, as the carved-up nature of the land means you can rarely just head anywhere directly. In some parts it looks like a miniature-scale version of one of those amazing national parks in Arizona, with the 'mountains' being not much bigger than people, and the 'canyons' being a bit of a squeeze to fit down.

There's accommodation out here too, for instance at El Cusco, where the lands get really bad — all kind of red and crazy — and goats, chickens and dogs roam around the farm-style accommodation.

The jumping off point for Desierto de Tatacoa is the town of Villavieja, an hour from the city of Neiva by minivan.

EVERYWHERE

Party at any Colombian festival, anywhere

It's all very well going around Colombia and visiting all these cool places but if you really want to get to know the country, you need to go beyond merely ticking off a series of geographical locations, and get to know the people. And a great way to get a feel for what Colombians are like is to experience one of the many festivals.

These are almost never your typical, humdrum, "Isn't that nice?" chin-stroking cultural events, but rather huge parties that take the form of street parades and other events right across the city. It's almost as though the 'thing' that the festival is celebrating (which could be flowers, jeeps, donkeys, or indeed pretty much anything) is an afterthought, and it's all just an elaborate excuse to have fun. That said, and as well as all the foam-spraying, cornflour-chucking mayhem, you'll almost inevitably get to learn something about one or more aspects of Colombian tradition simply by osmosis.

So pick a festival — any festival — and party like a mad thing with the locals. Try the Feria de Cali, the Feria de las Flores (Flower Festival) in Medellín, the Festival del Burro (Donkey Festival) in San Antero or the Yipao (Jeep Parade) in Armenia, or indeed any one of the other many, many options right across the country.

There's something on every month, so with a bit of planning, you should be able to enjoy the Colombian party spirit no matter when you're there. See the Wikipedia article on the subject to get a feel for what's on and when (http://bit.ly/1GpgRQL), then search for the organiser's specific page for the details. And do book your accommodation in advance if at all possible — when Colombians hold a party, everyone wants to be there.

Bonus — 10 More Things!

I've got 10 more suggestions of things to see and do in Colombia waiting for you online.

- More places!
- More activities!
- More exclamation marks and unnecessary hyperbole!

There are also photos, videos and all sorts of other stuff related to the items in this book.

To get access, simply sign up to my author mailing list (see below) and I'll send you the link immediately.

My mailing list is simply a way of keeping in touch with my readers. People on my list get access to special offers when they're available, and are also amongst the first to know when I bring out a new book.

Sign up here:
http://neilbennion.com/amazingcolombiareader

About the Author

Neil Bennion was born in 1974 in Lancashire, England. He's a writer and traveller who left a successful career in IT when he realised he much preferred prancing about in foreign countries to discussing technical scope changes. He blogs about travel, productivity and mucking about at wanderingdesk.com.

Also by this author:

Dancing Feat: One Man's Mission to Dance Like a Colombian (2014)

How to Learn to Dance in Colombia (2015)

There now follows a sample chapter of Dancing Feat: One Man's Mission to Dance Like a Colombian. Please be warned that it contains some bad language, and some even worse dancing (at least on my part)...

Chapter 1 — Danceless

"You dance like a twat."

I don't know what I was expecting to hear, but it definitely wasn't that. It was the morning after a night out in London's East End. We'd gone to a cool bar, had a few drinks and chucked a few shapes about. Except, according to my girlfriend of the time, mine looked like they'd been thrown by an amateur potter.

But that was all a long time ago now. And, besides, I solved the problem quite easily. Spurred on by my ex's comment, I went to dance classes and... no, wait: I just never danced with her again. Not for the entire remaining two years of the relationship.

Criticism is one of the great manipulators, and my dancing has been the subject of a lot of it over the years. The result has been that I've spent much of my adult life oscillating between someone who dances badly and someone who doesn't dance at all.

The thing is I came born with that natural English style, known as 'self-conscious, stiff-limbed awkwardness'. In this informal, well-adopted genre, changes to movement come with the same natural flow and spontaneity as the local-council planning permission process.

Legs aren't so bad: you can just do something repetitive with them, and they're mostly out of the line of sight. It's the arms that are the problem. The younger of my two sisters had a novel solution to this problem, appropriating some of the more emphatic and cooler-looking gestures she'd learnt in her sign language classes.

"There's a bomb! There's a bomb!" she would sign. "Get out! Get out!"

It's certainly a quick way of identifying all the deaf people in a club.

My own approach to dancing is to just tidy the arms away, where they can't do so much damage. This appears to be a common approach by rubbish dancers — store them permanently by the side, bent at the elbow. It's the same strategy adopted by the Tyrannosaurus Rex, a species which, incidentally, were also appalling dancers, and frequently mocked by the more able triceratops.

When it comes to dance, people will often say that you shouldn't care what people think; you should just get out there and enjoy yourself. This is great advice, especially if you have no desire to ever procreate. It's also the basis of one of the other styles of dance I subject the world to from time to time: over-expression. Lubricated by alcohol and enthusiasm, it's easy to get confused into thinking that because something feels good, it follows that it also looks good.

I've come to the conclusion that I must be like one of those talent show rejects that sings in unbridled joy, misreading the audience's reaction as an endorsement, with no-one having the heart to tell them that they're an object of derision. Unless they, too, have a brutally honest partner.

"You sing like a twat."

All four windows are wound-down partway, blasting me with lukewarm air. It dilutes the smells of the vehicle's interior: that of gasoline, aged-dustiness and the worn-out faux-leather seats that I'm sliding about on. I'm in Latin America alright — I could tell that with my eyes closed. Especially since I've just taken a flight there.

In the distance, a green chain of mountains rears up, corpulent and wrinkled; giant white loofahs in the sky for company. Somewhere between us and the mountains lies the city; behind us the airport is already just a memory.

We whistle along the concrete-sectioned highway, the radio filling the air with local rhythms. Some songs burst with rapid-fire beat clusters, whilst others are more lilting and gentle. Some sound bouncy and poppy, whilst others are slow and romantic. I can even tell some of them are cheesy, despite most of the lyrics being beyond the grasp of my so-so

Spanish. What I can't tell about any of the tracks is what type of music they are. They all just sound 'Latin'.

I adore music, which makes it all the more frustrating not being able to dance. You hear some music you love, and you feel that deep urge within to just... do... something. But for me this is where it all falls apart. I lack even the most basic vocabulary required for the interaction — I'm like a Labrador trying to discuss semiotics. So the great music plays on, and I just standing there barking. No, really.

A major part of this problem is the style of dancing I've grown up with. My parents, and their parents before them, used to go out and dance 'with' each other, which translated to some kind of physical contact. But I've grown up with the idea that dancing 'with' somebody else really means dancing 'at' them.

I feel like my generation has been kind of cheated: the only chance you have of a developing a real connection is by copying each other's actions, which can only be done ironically, or perhaps throwing in the odd wrestling hold. Okay, you can also make eye contact, though strangely enough women don't tend to give me much of that when I'm dancing.

So it would be great to learn how to dance properly.

That said, if I never managed it, it wouldn't be the end of the world, would it? In fact, it's entirely possible that I could just carry through my life as many other Englishmen have done, without ever learning to distinguish myself in that respect.

But there's another issue — I don't drink. It's been four years since I stopped — a consequence of a health problem I developed.

At first it was hellish. It was only when it was taken away that I realised how deeply ingrained alcohol had been into my life. Parties, dates and dinners; Birthdays, weddings and barbecues; Bonding with my dad; Watching sport; Lying in the gutter mumbling incoherently — every social activity, big or small, had alcohol at its core. And every single one was now awkward.

Even the pub, so long an amber-toned refuge from the harshness of life, was transformed into a land of sodden beermats and shouty people. Whilst nightclubs suddenly seemed pointless.

But you can get used to pretty much anything given enough time. I became comfortable — happy even — going out at night, weaving non-judgementally around the pavement vomit of Manchester, giving the staggerers and fight-starters a respectful distance.

More than just getting used to it, I began to flourish. Not drinking forced me to seek out all sorts of alternatives to fill the vacated space. I learnt how to meditate and I learnt how to massage (well, how to pay for a massage). I took a greater interest in cultural events, cinema and scientific scepticism. I found myself seeking new and interesting things to do of an evening instead of always reaching for a glass. In short, it enriched me.

But despite all I've gained, there is still something missing from my evenings. Out-and-out, mind-blowing hedonism is probably always going to be out of reach, but I need something else. I need a way of letting go. I need fun, excitement and anticipation. I need a focus for the evening other than just the repeated pouring of liquids in the general direction of the oesophagus.

None of the alternatives I've tried have matched up. Joining language clubs, going bowling, stealing cars — they're all good social activities, but none of them quite hits the mark. And there are only so many games of naked Twister you can propose before people stop answering your calls.

And that's where we come back to dance. For here is an activity which allows people to reach great heights of self-expression and make them feel alive. An activity which, at its extreme, is nothing less than an exploration of ecstasy and a baring of the soul, yet which can be done casually with friends, too.

(You're right, that's begging for a joke.)

It's something that's actually good for you if you know what you're doing, and something which previous girlfriends have complained I couldn't do properly. Something that doing in a state of sobriety seems like madness (indeed there are those who claim they've never done it sober).

(Okay, I'll stop now.)

I need dance in my life.

There's another potential upside to this. Due to a mixture of incompetence, too much time at the writing desk and the side-effects of not drinking, I've somehow found myself in my mid-thirties and without a woman in my life to call my long-term partner. It's disappointing — I thought I'd have been trapped in a loveless marriage for years by now.

Dance seems like a great way for men to meet women. Not least because if we've agreed to clasp onto each other for three to five minutes then at least I've got some kind of a sales window. Actually forget meeting women — I'm just going to use it to sell conservatories to strangers.

Back in the here and now, the cityscape at the base of the mountains begins to loom, and soon we're on its fringes, joined at a distance by commercial new-builds and modern apartment blocks. The scent of cut grass blows in from well-maintained reservations — the smell of investment — and soon we've reached the outer limits of a spanking-new guided bus system.

Spanish is everywhere, streaming out of the radio, directing traffic and selling products. Not that it's always necessary: as the road changes from highway to street, shops appear with images of their wares hand-painted directly on the wall. Hardware stores have images of hammers and bed shops have images of beds. I wonder what they paint on the outside of brothels.

I saw a lot of this kind of thing (hand-painted signs more than brothels) on my previous journey to Latin America, so I know this is quite normal here.

I must admit, though, I'm still seduced by the idea we are sold in the UK of what Latin America, or at least Latin spirit, looks like. I'm thinking specifically of those white rum adverts with their compelling narratives of open-air partying and sultry Latin chicas. But then I've seen some of the reality of nights out in this part of the world, too, and it's still pretty impressive.

I've stood periscope-like on a dance floor full of Bolivians wondering how they all just seemed to know what to do — public information films, perhaps? I've been to bars in South America and seen even the stiffest-looking office worker soften their shoulders at the merest hint of Latin music and begin casually gyrating where they stood. And I've seen dancing on the Caribbean coast of Central America that looked closer to sex than, well, sex.

But some countries have stronger dance cultures than others. Indeed, there's one in particular that I've heard a lot about over the years — a country that would probably be famous for its dance and music were it not famous for other things first. It's a country whose reputation precedes it. It's also a country I've never been to. Until today, that is.

The taxi driver has his seat pushed right forward to compensate for his own lack of height, creating masses of space in front of me and making him look really eager. I'm willing to bet he could not only name every type of music coming out of his radio, but could also dance to each one of them without a second thought, too.

The traffic thickens and the buildings begin to close in and rise up. Some look only a few decades old, but are already beyond tired, whilst others, I'm guessing from the 1920s and 30s, have a semi-modern elegance, redolent of rolodexes and yellowing memos. They're not ancient, but they've certainly been around a while.

Not unlike myself, really. I'm still relatively young, but time is marching on. The years are speeding up. Blink and I'll be 40 (I don't know what'll happen if I wink). At some point you start to realise that all those things that you thought you would get round to at some point ... well you really might want to start getting round to them. And dance is one of those things.

I've put this off far too long already. I don't want to dance self-consciously anymore, nor over-expressively. I don't want to dance any variation on a theme of 'twat'. I want to dance well. I want people to look at me and say "He might be a twat in many and varied ways, but you wouldn't know it to watch him dance."

I want to be able to dance with a partner instead of at her; to share that thing; to connect in that way. I want to be able to say "Shall we dance" without an unsaid "individually, but relatively near" appended to the end.

I want women to be attracted to the way I dance; to find it appealing; to smile at me out of a sense of connection rather than pity. I don't want to be a solitary old man, sat all alone growing more and more right wing. I want to grow more and more right wing with someone I love.

I want a way of socialising with people beyond just a shared inability to form coherent sentences. I want something to look forward to at weekends; a reason to get out from behind my writing desk; a way of letting go and actually having some fun.

I want to have the guts to get on the dance floor at all, instead of having a dance confidence that's so brittle that I'd rather pretend to be deaf and charge out of the club under instruction from my younger sister than actually lay some moves down.

I want to be able to dance, dammit. That's where I'm at. Is that really too much to ask?

The rough green fabric of the mountains is closing in now, the city gently rising on its hem. We're nearly there. The driver takes a turn crosstown and the buildings take a turn for the historic. Squat, colonial-style edifices with rendered walls and red roof tiles suddenly dominate. They look like a mashed-up packet of crayons: bright green with pink mouldings; orange with blue mouldings; yellow with red mouldings. Back home, if you painted your house a bright colour you'd be considered an idiot. Here, you could be as expressive as you like and you'd be lucky if anyone noticed.

As for my own expressive shortcomings, if I'm going to address them then I want to do it properly. You can take dance classes everywhere these days. But I have a need for adventure to fulfil, too. Travel is in my blood (and, as a result, parasites are often in my intestines). I need to move, explore, discover; to go to places that excite me; to yield to that part of the soul that can only be sated by having one's photo taken in front of foreign landmarks.

The thought of taking the odd class once a week with — I don't know — 'Salsa Dave' doesn't inspire or motivate me. Forget the substitute: I want to go straight to the source.

I want a piece of the life that rum adverts push — a real slice of hot Latin action. I want to go where rhythm is in the blood, where the street is a dance floor, and where you can get into trouble for the ownership of powdered milk (like British politician Michael Fabricant).

I want to go to a place I've never been before, in search of something I've never had.

I want to dance like a Colombian.

Dancing Feat

Dancing Feat is the hilarious travel memoir about one man's mission to dance like a Colombian. It's available now in paperback and ebook — http://amzn.to/1odeSVE

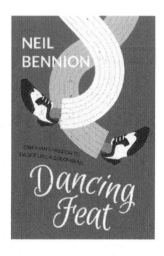

"Unmissable! A beacon of inspiration for all wannabe dancers."

"Dancing Feat will spur feelings of both wanderlust and dancerlust."

"Thoroughly recommended if you're interested in dance or Colombia, but also very funny book in its own right"

"Apart from being very funny, I felt really absorbed by the culture and warmth of this fascinating country and its people. It's a great read!"

"Informative, interesting but most of all hilarious."